You Are The
Artist Of Your
OWN Life.
Don't hand The
PaintbRush TO
Anyone else.

Annette

AND Book

Amanda Haigh

Published in 2021

Copyright 2021 Amanda Haigh

Authors: Amanda Haigh, Amanda Burton, Rob Neary, Susan Hanley, Bernadette Spellman, Joe Booth, Annette Probets, Sally Pater, Ashley , Bhupesh Limbachia, Colleen Ward.

Photography: Jan Wells

Disclaimer: AND is intended for information and education purposes only. This book does not constitute specific advice to your situation. The views and opinions expressed in this book are those of the author and do not reflect those of the editor or copyright holder. All people mentioned in the chapters have been used with permission.   To the best of my knowledge the author has complied with fair usage. Future editions can be rectified if ommissions are brought to authors attention.

ACKNOWLEDGEMENT

I would like to thank the amazing entrepreneurs and staff team who has been a part of making AND such a special business and their beautiful stories told within this book.

Each entrepreneur working on AND have contributed to making this brand such a success and are so passionate about making the lives of autistic and learning-disabled adults the best they can be.

I would also like to make a special thank you to Jan Wells who has followed the AND brand from the beginning and done the film and photo shoot which has been displayed in the book.

I hope you all enjoy reading.

TABLE OF CONTENT

CHAPTER 1

Photo credit: Jan Wells

I wanted to write this book so that we can raise the profile of the extremely talented and amazing people I have the pleasure in working with, from our members, entrepreneurs, trainees right through to our dedicated staff team. We all work hard to give a voice to learning-disabled and autistic adults, and this is how we do it......

My name is Amanda Haigh and I manage this wonderful self-advocacy service and absolutely love my job with a passion. I have always wanted to showcase learning-disabled adults' talents to the world the same way that I have come to love working alongside them. There are so many talented learning-disabled and autistic people with lots of great skills who inspire me every day. They are non-judgemental people who I have learnt so much from and this has transferred into my own life.

Unfortunately for this community, lockdown has shed a light on the many inequalities that they face, these have been there for a long time, but lockdown exacerbated this, especially with the huge digital divide. Leep1 was lucky in the fact that we embraced digital a few years before lockdown struck and used tablets within our lessons as we knew how important it was to get this community online and using tech, so they weren't left behind. I am aware this was a struggle for other services who weren't using technology and not as far advanced as Leep1. It worked in Leep1's favour as in March 2020 we were able to deliver tablets to our members and deliver an online service via Facebook to stop them from being isolated and keep them in touch with our service for extra support. We delivered a full timetable, food safety, yoga, healthy living, scam awareness, digital skills and some of the members do DJ sets on an evening. It really has been the most amazing community that came together in a time of need, now with numbers of 391 group members, one from Singapore.

During my 10 years working at Leep1 I have set up various social enterprises in response to our learning-disabled members by listening to what their needs are and responding by applying for funding and setting up meaningful and purposeful activities that are run by and for them.

Our members wanted a club night in the city centre once a month, the only other night ran twice yearly and was held in a university. Our club night began in 2013 at Tiger Tiger and when this shut down in the city, we moved to Pryzm a night club which is also in the heart of the city centre. The club night is absolutely loved by people with learning disabilities and autism across Leeds and beyond, which over 200 people attend. Here we did our very first launch of the clothing and had some beautiful models showcasing the first ever prototype of the AND brand. The Mayor of Leeds came along to open the show alongside Susan Hanley our co-chair of Leep1. Two great councillors from Leeds were also in attendance Councillor Ritchie and Councillor Khan who came to watch the show and are always supportive of what we do. Councillor Ritchie is a learning disability champion and campaigns to make change for learning-disabled adults in Leeds. He also co-chairs the 'Being Safe' task group which is a strand of the 'Being Me' strategy in Leeds, helping to make the lives of learning-disabled people the best and safest possible.

One of the models from the fashion show, Michael

Our members told us that there were not many employment opportunities for learning disabled and autistic adults, so I set up Cafe Leep which is an accredited employment training cafe supporting adults with learning disabilities into employment. Through the café we have got 13 learning-disabled and autistic adults into employment and 32 through the NVQ accreditation process. The café went on to be the heart and soul of Leep1 with Angie managing the café and Darren the NVQ trainer successfully putting the trainees through the accreditation process and winning the best café in Yorkshire and Humber in 2017.

Angie - Café Manager, Darren - NVQ Trainer, Joe – Café Leep paid employee and one of the AND entrepreneurs   Photo Credit: Shy Shamila Burton

One of our members was a victim of mate crime, she was befriended by a couple in the pub, they took her money and her card when they invited her to their home after a few drinks and became abusive towards her.

Mate crime is a hard crime to recognise for learning-disabled adults due to them wanting to make friends with people easily. They often struggle to recognise whether people are fake or real friends. Mate crime is a devious crime, one which the perpetrator pretends to be the victim's friend for their own personal gain, taking advantage of the person's kindness to their own detriment. Because of this we run campaigns in schools (year 6 primary) to raise hate/mate crime awareness through forum theatre alongside a theatre group called Bright Sparks.

Watch the YouTube clip of our performers and why we are passionate about stopping hate and mate crimes, put your camera on your phone and scan the QR code.

Below are our performers, Tauseef, Olivia and Susan

LEEP1's primary expertise is a deep understanding of the needs of learning-disabled adults and supporting them to develop independent lives. We set up a clothing brand with a social purpose, the mission is to change the way the world views learning-disabled adults, tackling the stigma and inequalities they face. AND Clothes is an enterprise run by and for adults with learning disabilities. We support our team members to learn business skills, develop entrepreneurial talent, build confidence, and help them have the lives they choose. All the clothing designs are created by our entrepreneurs, emblazoned with empowering slogans and phrases. 100% of our profits go back into building a brand our team can be proud of.

YouTube clip featuring the AND entrepreneurs, produced by the talented Jan Wells.

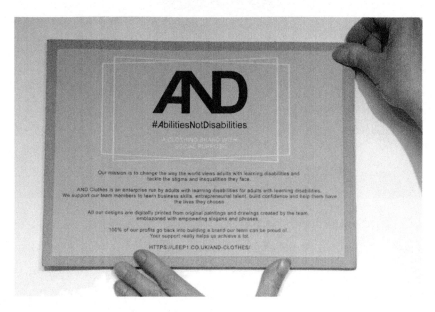

photo credit: Jan Wells

Susan, our chair of Leep1 a lady with Downs Syndrome, who I will talk about in chapter 2, has a passion for design and fashion and she wanted to be able to design her own brand supporting adults with learning disabilities to understand entrepreneurship.

She got together with 8 entrepreneurs with learning disabilities and autism and with the help of some funding through the Health Trust enabled Leep1 to start the clothing brand. They had been planning the brand behind the scenes, looking at the meaning and design for the AND logo, prior to setting up the business. Rebecca Hainsworth who is the deputy manager at Leep1 asked her cousin 'Ryan Burns' who is very artistic and creative to come up with some designs, he did several and then we asked the team which one they preferred. With the Health Trust funding we were able to pay for staff resource and give this community the chance to learn all about entrepreneurship, running an online business with an amazing logo to match, the rest is history.

The AND Entrepreneur programme is being led and taught by an inspirational artist, Amanda Burton who has just won 'The Creative Award' for her work over lockdown with Leep1. She began working with Leep1 in Café Leep and when lockdown struck, we saw another side to Amanda's talents which was her amazing artistic flare and attention to detail. We knew she would be the right person to run the AND project and we were right. Since her redeployment she has been working alongside our newly appointed staff member, employed in lockdown, who is autistic and has also got an artistic flare, both are whizzes on photo shop and together they are working beside our AND entrepreneurs to create a sellable clothing label. Between them they have taken the AND label to another level. You can hear more about Rob in chapter 4.

The eight entrepreneurs who have a love for art have been involved through each process of the set-up and they wanted to develop and direct the business over the next year so that it becomes self-sustainable, enabling us to offer more essential life skills to many more learning disabled and autistic adults. We are hoping the clothing brand AND will leave a lifetime legacy in changing the public's perception of learning-disabled adults. With the AND brand we want to make a world that becomes more inclusive of autistic and learning-disabled adults and any other differences, be it race, gender, religion, everyone has 'abilities' to contribute to today. There are so many hidden talents out there, people need to think about the wider picture, work together and make the changes needed for an equal and inclusive society with everyone adding to the jigsaw puzzle.

The AND business helps with many areas for a learning-disabled and autistic person. Digital Skills, Entrepreneurship, Employment skills, modelling, and becoming their own artists for the clothing which is all done by hand and then their artwork is developed digitally and put onto clothing and merchandise. Each entrepreneur is stronger in different areas, one has a love for social media marketing, one has a love for modelling, one a love for art and already has the confidence to call herself an artist.

The brand can open various career paths that the entrepreneurs could take when the course ends and each one has their own specialist area. Because they are so different in their skill sets the eight entrepreneurs work so well together as a team while focussing on their area of interest.

More recently, the entrepreneurs found by putting their new designs online that there was a need for a more digital inclusive shopping experience. The AND team are working alongside a global app developer called Dubit to produce an accessible safe shopping app. Dubit is a kids research agency and digital development studio, that helps create #1 products for global brands and innovative start-ups.

With offices in Leeds, London, Washington DC and Melbourne, Dubit have world class teams that deliver at every stage of the journey, from initial ideation, through design and development, to launch strategy.   The name of the organisation came from their original development of a debit card for pupils to use with their lunch money called a Dubit Card.

The app will work in several ways, it will allow them to shop online safely, knowing that via the app the website will be a safe one to shop on and allow them to budget. Along with the app they will have a card that they will pre-upload with cash. This can limit their spending so that they can start learning how to budget effectively in a risk-free way. Finally, all eight entrepreneurs will be designing the app as they are the people with lived experience. The AND group have learned about commercial design, sourcing of appropriate raw materials and the supply chain. As well as design and entrepreneurial skills, our LEEP1 members would be available to conduct focus groups to help diagnose app development needs and interface experience with the app. The app will open so many doors for the disabled community.

Through our contact with Leeds University and the Positive Impact Partnership programme (connecting universities to third sector organisations) we have had the pleasure and support of a wonderful Associate Professor from the university called Pammi Sinha, she has been super committed to helping us with the brand, with support from her students and through this partnership we have become part of FFF Future Fashion Factory. Future Fashion Factory is a £5.4 million R&D partnership exploring and developing new digital and advanced **textile** technologies to boost the design of high-value creative products. Innovation Future Fashion Factory tackles some of the biggest challenges facing the fashion and **textiles** industry and AND clothes are honoured to be amongst some of the world leaders.

Here we will be able to pilot the app amongst the other cohort members, Including, ASOS, Burberry, M & S and Fabrication. Fabrication is where our AND clothing is sold which is situated in the heart of Leeds city centre. Fabrication is a shop for independent artists across Leeds and we partner with them to sell the clothes on their online platform and in the shop. This will also allow our entrepreneurs work experience in a retail setting and have visibility within the city centre.

In lockdown we were part of the UnLtd thrive programme and they introduced us to Patrick Grant. Susan was overwhelmed to have the pleasure of meeting him as she always watches The Great British Sewing Bee. He runs a clothing brand called Community Clothing which is also part of the FFF cohort. It was great to get some sound advice from him as he has been part of the fashion industry for many years. He also mentioned that he absolutely loved Susan's design which was a take on Van Gogh's famous art piece, emblazoned with stAND Together, a clever use of the AND logo within the wording STAND.

Having the app will enable more spending from the disabled community, **The 'purple pound'** is a term that describes the spending power of disabled people and their families.

Do disabled people have much spending power?

The UK's 11.9 million disabled people are said to have disposable income collectively worth £80bn. Campaign groups regularly cite this figure and find it useful to remind businesses and politicians that disabled people are a sizeable economic force and should not be forgotten. Disability consultant Mary-Anne Rankin says that businesses should think inclusively from the very beginning of any product or service they're starting. She says: "You've got to think about the widest possible usage of your services and explore innovative ways of enabling everybody to benefit from them. Because after all if your customers can benefit, you're going to make more money." The BBC News said **scan to read the full report**

It will be hugely profitable for online businesses if the disabled community are able to access the internet in a safe way and can shop online.

We would like to set up a big campaign to make websites more accessible for all the community to use.

A report from Scope (above) has identified clothes shopping to be second highest problematic online shopping area (after groceries) and have said 98% of websites are un-accessible. Joe one of the entrepreneurs said, "That's 98% too much" and rightly so. The digital divide is a huge issue and even more so since the pandemic, having an app like this potentially helps many that are vulnerable and isolated by being able to shop online as everyone else does. A benefit of learning to shop independently supports other aspects of independent living such as budgeting, improving confidence and other essential life skills needed in their daily lives.

Scan the QR code to read the Scope report

LEEP1's approach has always been one of empowerment; by engaging its members in the development of the app will boost their sense of ownership of the issues and their solutions and build confidence to develop entrepreneurial aspirations. Thus, making it accessible for learning-disabled adults to become more independent and learn how to take control of their own finances.

Our entrepreneurs recently did their first photo shoot which was awesome, we went into Leeds city centre looking for some great back drops for the pictures. You can see below in some of the pictures how much their confidence went through the roof at this shoot. It so lovely to see how the eight have formed such a tight bond already and we can't wait to get back to having all eight together again at once, because the bond really formed online over Zoom.

When they met again for the photo shoot you could see what a tight nit group they all are. Even Rob our newest member of staff, he tells his story in chapter 4, has told us how his confidence has grown as a person too, especially as an adult who has autism, but our mission is to help everyone succeed and make AND the best brand.

It's incredible to hear even Amanda who leads on the project (chapter 3) has witnessed the change in the team and even her attitude to people with learning disabilities has brought her confidence and artistic flare to rise once again.

Having that peer support amongst them and not having a hierarchy just makes the cogs turn beautifully for everyone.

Photo credit - Jan Wells

In the picture above Bhupesh one of entrepreneurs who has a love for Indian

design. His design is modelled by the lovely Colleen on the next page.

Photo credits: Jan Wells

We have had some incredible reviews on our Facebook page about the clothing brand and we can't wait to scale up the business to offer many more designs and support more learning-disabled adults to become entrepreneurs.

We are hoping that the first year of trading will allow us to employ more people with learning disabilities running the AND clothes brand, supporting the next cohort in 2022. Our plan is to employ a member from the first cohort of 2021 so they can expand their development further. We would love to be able to change publics perceptions of learning-disabled adults through the label #AbilitiesNotDisabilities globally, raising awareness of the amazing learning-disabled talent and what variety and impact they can bring to organisations through employing them and giving them the chance to shine.

Our long-term goal is to sell enough clothing to keep offering business support to many more learning-disabled adults and to be able to employ 50% within the AND team by 2023.

Because people with learning disabilities and/or autism are furthest away from the labour market, employment will be even harder to find after the Covid-19 pandemic. Many were or still are isolated due to the current pandemic and many still don't have the required digital skills to get online, learning the social media aspect of the course helps support their online skills to improve but more importantly raises their profile and improves their confidence.

The digital divide is huge but luckily Leeds is one of the leaders in joining forces to make this change. Leep1 is part of ALaDDIN which stands for Autism and Learning Disability Digital Inclusion Network it is a large group of organisations fighting to close the gap.

Leep1 did a consultation which was with 5 people from across the ALaDDIN networks with varying digital skills so we could look at different areas such as, did they use the internet and if so, what for? They also looked at different apps, safe shopping, scams. Only 1 person in the group knew that the padlock symbol on the top left resembled a safe sight, also this feature is only small and not recognisable in that format. This community need something they can see instantly, using a clear, large, and recognisable symbol.

Scan for digital inclusion survey

CHAPTER 2
WHERE IT ALL BEGAN......

Photo credit: Jan Wells

Allow me to introduce myself...

I'm Susan Hanley, I'm 56 years old and I have Downs Syndrome.

Born and brought up in Leeds, I went to school in West Ardsley, it has a swimming pool and we used to do music lessons, Physical Education, learn how to tell the time, and drama. Then I went to college at Park Lane annexe for people with a learning disability - I learnt lots of new skills there including drama.

I've always been interested in knitting and needlework, having watched my mum and Aunty who were both passionate about crafts and they taught me crocheting. When I crochet it takes me to my happy place and I feel like they are beside me again like the old times, it gives me comfort. I love making things like blankets, patch work. I was a very happy child, and I had a Golden Retriever called Bess and a white rabbit called Bright Eyes and Snowy, I kept giving him different names, whatever I felt like at the time. The first skills I learnt was embroidery, but I can't remember how that started or who taught me that skill.

I also went to West Ardsley training centre where I explored more Drama, Art, Needlework and created a small café just for tea, coffee, and biscuits.

My dad's name was Harold Hanley, he loved to play golf at Pudsey and my mums name was Elizabeth-Mary Hanley, she died when I was 17. She always had curlers in her hair, and I used to make her a cup of tea on a morning.

After she died, I went to live with my eldest sister Jacqueline. I have two sisters and one brother. I did lots of new things, like going to a dance class called 'Kids for Kids', and 2 youth clubs called 'Pudsey Gateway Club' and 'Lewisham Park' in Morley.

I had one best friend from school and I'm now in Leep1 with her so it's great to keep in contact. My favourite music was Lena Zavaroni, Abba and Val Doonican and I used to sing along to them.

I've been Co-Chair of Leep1 for 11 years, a self-advocacy organisation for people with Learning Disabilities. I've been there since the beginning, learning lots of new skills and gaining lots of confidence in myself and my work.

I am now an Ambassador for people with Learning Disabilities in Leeds, as well as an Ambassador for Safeguarding. I provide Learning Disability Awareness training to different organisations, including the commissioners at Leeds City Council, the police and volunteers and students. In lockdown I trained over 72 police officers and I had great feedback they were very impressed with the Presentation. I was involved in a campaign about "Get Me" which involved trying to get people with a Learning Disability to be recognised in society.

I have been featured on lots of media, one of the most famous was on BBC Breakfast news when I did a film clip around women with disabilities often going through the menopause earlier than other women, which is usually around the age of 50. I thought it was important to tell students who were studying to become GP's or nurses, so I could spread awareness and I have trained them around this in the past. You can find this on our YouTube page Leep1.

I am good at creating things and have a website called 'Creative Hands'. I teach other people with a Learning Disability how to knit, embroidery and do tapestry. I am always making things and my work was showcased on a display in Leeds City Museum. Seeing my work displayed in public made me very proud and I was able to open the display and talk about it to everyone on the opening night. If I feel stressed doing my needlework helps me to relax.

I am so excited about the AND project, especially now we have launched our new designs we all created together. Our AND clothing range is sold either online or at a shop in Leeds city centre called Fabrication. We are also in the process of setting up a platform on Ebay.

In the future I want to do more self-advocacy training, because "nothing about us, without us!", I would also like to do more learning disability awareness presentations to the public to get our voices heard. I want to have a stand at public events to promote the AND range so people can see what we can do, not what we can't do!

Photo credit: Jan Wells

I do a regular weekly podcast inviting people with learning disabilities to talk about their skills called 'Empower Me' which really highlights the brilliant talents of the learning-disabled communities. I invite other self-advocates from across the UK to speak and get their voices heard.

Together with the AND team, we want to change public's perception of learning-disabled adults to see what they can do, not what they can't. Together, with our brand (AND - #AbilitiesNotDisabilities) we will make this change.

I would love to become an MP one day and fight for the rights of more learning-disabled adults where I can get my voice heard and we are properly represented in society.

CHAPTER 3

AMANDA BURTON

How Art Changed My Life

Born in Malaysia in the seventies I enjoyed the hot climate and all the colourful and exotic creatures that lived in the tropics. As a child I played for hours catching butterflies (even snakes!) and spent nearly all my time outdoors exploring nature which I was fascinated by. I enjoyed arts and crafts, but it was never encouraged or nurtured. I believe every child is born a creative, but with a Malaysian mother who did not enjoy the privileges of an education and a British Engineer as a father it was mapped out for me that I should pursue a career in medicine or the sciences like the rest of my family. It was clear that academia and not a career in the arts was where I was heading.

However, my heart was always with art. I really enjoyed art class at school, but I was terrified of the Art teacher Mr Rigby, as a shy 13-year-old I found him to be a very eccentric man, strict and always full of criticism. It was at sixth form college when I really discovered I had some talent for drawing and painting, and I studied it as an extra-curricular activity alongside my A levels. I was so envious of the art students who were studying the A Level.

So, I studied Biochemistry at Leeds University with a view to move into Forensics. I used to joke with my friends that I would be the 'real life' Forensic Pathologist Amanda Burton from Silent Witness. However, I struggled a great deal at university, always nervous and insecure, I lacked greatly in confidence and self-assertiveness. Making the move from Malaysia was a big upheaval, along with many other challenges I faced as a child. I know now this was the onset of further mental health difficulties that were to come.

I had my first nervous breakdown when I was just 21 – just after the death of my father – and after receiving quite invasive ECT treatment I was left with little memory or concentrating ability. I was then diagnosed with a mental health condition and was told I would never recover; I would never work again, and my nerves were permanently damaged. After being given my 'label' I felt shamed, and stigma and my mental health condition became my sole identity. I let it consume my whole outlook on life for several years.

I would often sit and paint in watercolours or try different arts and crafts to pass the time. In my time away from employment I studied interior design, pottery, and visual merchandising. Even after winning a national achievement award - The Bronze Medal from the British Display Society of Window Dressers I still lacked the confidence and belief in myself and turned down a jet setting lifestyle designing windows for large department stores in Europe.

In my late thirties I started to volunteer for an Art Centre that had just opened that supported people with mental health issues, and I co-founded and developed the service alongside another artist. I was offered the job as Arts Development Worker and it was here, after being surrounded by other creatives and forming connections with the art world, that I really began to take art seriously. My own practice really developed becoming much more conceptual and I would try push the boundaries of what I was capable of, but also what innovative materials and techniques could be used to make art.

My scientific past plays a huge part in my creative thinking and style. I am a natural problem solver; I love to experiment and invent new ways of working so I started using materials such as candle smoke to paint and draw with. My other passion is making jewellery and in 2007 my work was featured in Vogue Magazine and I was invited to exhibit at the Chelsea Flower Show. It was ironic that after years of rejecting science in 2010 one of my paintings was chosen to be an academic book cover for Ecological Studies at Harvard University.

So, after years of self-struggle I had entered the world of art and creativity. I had finally found my new identity as an artist– I was now filled with more confidence, self-esteem, purpose and finally felt I was playing a worthwhile part in society. I had come a long way from the damaged lost individual I was after my ECT.

I felt compelled to share and teach others how art could really change the way you feel about yourself, provide you with a positive sense of identity and make you feel part of a wider community. Not only is the practice of doing art therapeutic and relaxing which is great for your mental health but the mindset of problem solving, focussing on solutions and creative thinking is a positive mental space to be in. I worked in the arts and mental health field for over ten years and became practiced in helping people develop as individuals and artists.

In 2020 I joined Café Leep1 as I wanted a change in career and really wanted to work alongside adults with learning disabilities. During Covid, only a few months into my contract, I was redeployed into a more creative role and I helped to shape the AND project as lead artist. I was so excited by what the possibilities were, and I was thrilled I could share my passion for art, and it's benefits with others.

AND Clothes not only has a strong purpose, but our team has a unique way of working together. I have never come across anything so positive before. The mutual support and encouragement to and from each member is truly inspiring to be a part of. All business decisions are made as a team; there is no hierarchy, only real respect for one another, valuing each other's skills and ideas. Some of the team focus on marketing, art and design or excel in encouraging others. Everyone has an important and valued role to play which contributes to the strong symbiotic success of the group. Society really has a lot to learn from people who have learning disabilities about how to be kind, work with and respect one another. I learn a lot from my students, and I hope they learn as much from me.

I love to see how the team become so engaged with the project and doing the art. The designs so far have been full of unlimited imagination and amazing skill. Some of the members have already enquired about other areas they can study such as fashion design and Graffiti Art and I love to think that this project could be opening more doors and opportunities for everyone. One of my students has told me they now identify themselves as an artist – which if the journey and mindset becomes like my own - I can't wait to see him and more of the group flourish into confident and empowered individuals they can and should be.

The AND team really identify themselves as a tight unified team and being part of this group, working towards one mission together is giving a real sense of community and purpose. Together we will tackle the inequalities people with learning disabilities face – that is our mission. However, self-confidence, self-belief and self-esteem I believe are also the keys in being able to take steps towards personal goals and a future of your choosing. The space and time we spend together making art and running the business is a positive nurturing environment so everyone can flourish. I am incredibly proud of every single one of the team, their positive attitude, devotion, and spirit is what drives us forwards and makes me love what I do so much.

CHAPTER 4

ROB NEARY – AND PROJECT SUPPORT WORKER

I grew up in a seaside town in North Wales called Rhyl. I lived there with my parents and 2 older brothers. They moved from Paisley in Scotland when I was still growing in my mother's womb. I've 2 nephews and have loved being an uncle. I also have a younger sister, but we lost her soon after she was born. Unfortunately, home wasn't always the easiest place to be. There was often arguing and shouting. When I was 7, my mum became sick with Cushing's Syndrome and that continued for a period of around 2 years. All the while I had built up problems with anger - getting in trouble for breaking things, fighting with my brothers, or just generally 'kicking off'. In school, however, I always tried to pay attention and listen but often struggled to understand and hold the information that I was being taught, as well as staying focused on tasks. I was very shy and struggled to ask for help so found ways to cope and figure things out for myself. I progressed to high school where many of the same problems continued and I put my schoolwork on the backburner in place of trying to fit in with my peers, getting myself into situations I didn't want or expect to be in. My 'friends' often excluded me on one hand and insisted on me doing things they wanted or expected from me on the other. Outside of school, I loved to play football and competed in kung fu & kickboxing. I excelled at sports, playing football for the North Wales representative team and Rhyl FC in the Welsh Academies Premier League, and competed in the British Opens for Kung Fu & Kickboxing at 14, placing 2nd against older competitors. Fighting in the ring was where I felt most at home, and as I improved so did my self-esteem and confidence in my own ability to achieve something. I went to college at 16 to study Public Services as I wanted to work in the emergency services, where I also played football for the college team. Again, experiencing difficulties with confidence and socialising with others, I distanced myself from sports altogether once I had finished college. My parents finally got divorced, and I took on responsibilities at home. After a year and a half, I moved on to university in Leeds to study International Relations & Peace Studies. I moved with my girlfriend, having met when we were in school at 15. We loved each other's company so much that we knew we wanted to take on life together, so that's what we did. At university, I finally realised my abilities in academic writing and research and my confidence in my reading and writing improved as I found myself deep into my books. I continued to struggle socially throughout and blamed myself each time I tried and failed to push myself, so my mental health took a big knock – I constantly questioned why I was this way and regularly fell into bouts of depression, growing in anxiety, self-harming and taking drugs. Regardless of this, I set out to prove to myself that if I put in the effort, I could achieve anything that I set out to achieve. I did and graduated in 2016 from my degree with a 2:1 grade. In the years since, I've been in and out of jobs for one reason or another. I landed a graduate job in which I had the task of improving the student experience at a university, in which I excelled. It was while working in this role that I attended a day course on working with Autistic students in Higher Education. Listening to the speakers and learning, more and more of what was being taught resonated inside me and I had a big 'lightbulb moment'. I had so many questions that I felt needed answers, so I sought medical advice and was eventually diagnosed as being Autistic at 24. It took time to understand fully what this meant, and I still had so many questions about myself, and I guess I'm still figuring some of this out, but in time it has brought about the chance to accept myself for who I am. I still struggle with what exactly Autism *is*, as the experience is lived so differently by so many fellow autistic people, but what I do understand is that we are different to what is expected in the social world and that these differences are often not accepted whether through misunderstanding or ignorance – I hope to make a difference and challenge the ideas held by so many through education and raising awareness. I don't yet know how that might look, but I know it's needed for so many. Since diagnosis, I've attempted to start numerous businesses in design – 2 main ventures being my fashion brand "Neanderthal" and an upcycled furniture and design company "Dis.Organised", launching both during the Lockdown during 2020. Although it's been a real challenge to learn so many new skills, I've loved creating and seeing people appreciate what I've made. I continue to take steps in my own life to improve my mental health and have recently started taking up sports and exercise again.

In December 2020, I started my new role as a Project Support Worker with the AND project and have been welcomed by my new team with open arms. I've had moments of strength, weakness, and times where I've felt I just couldn't do anything. But having a team around me that never gives up, remains positive throughout the toughest of times and just simply get the job done has been refreshing and inspiring to me, and I've finally found the courage to communicate the things that I have struggled with. Mandy and Amanda have been encouraging and have listened, and they have shown me that people will go to great lengths to help – and I think the world could do with a lot more people with the compassion and understanding they have shown me. I cannot wait to see where this project leads the team and hope to see my team continue to grow in confidence and take their own leaps in their lives. Together, the AND team are showing what people with Learning Disabilities can achieve when given the chance to shine.

Chapter 5

Bhups 'the Bob Marley' – and Entrepreneur

I grew up in Bradford, I was born in St. Luke's Hospital. I started at Lidget Green nursery when I was three, it was a special needs nursery. After that I moved to Gipton and my dad bought his first paper and grocery shop in Middleton and then went on to buy one in Gipton. I remember this because I celebrated my third birthday party and we also celebrated him buying the shop. I went to special needs Wykebeck primary school in Gipton, I didn't like this school because I used to get bullied. They used racist comments toward me and made fun of my disability. I had an Indian tuition teacher who helped me with my maths and English. I didn't have any friends there which made me upset, and they used to tease me about the fact I couldn't write or tell the time.

After that I went to Temple Moore High school, I didn't like this school either because they made fun out of my hair which was long at the time. They called me smelly Paki and made fun of my culture. I used to get beaten up by a couple of kids in the same class as me and the headteacher put me in another class to keep me away from the bullies. I didn't like this school, I was once pushed into the swimming pool and into the cubicles and had the door slammed in my face causing me to bust my head and then I had to go to hospital.

After this I went to Thomas Danby for five years and I enjoyed it there. I made lots of friends and my best friend was called Roger. I learnt computer skills, business studies, English, and maths and I passed GCSE in 2000. I left college being able to tell the time properly and felt very proud of this achievement.

In 2003 my dad passed away, my family phoned my tutor called Carol and they took me to the hospital to see my dad as he was on a life support machine. My mum wrote a letter to my teacher so that I could go to India to spread his ashes in the River Ganges. I was there for eight weeks in total, and I celebrated my 21st birthday at the same time.

I lived with my mum, dad and two sisters, one of my sisters called Jetexa got married and I was the best man. This was not an arranged marriage but was through them falling in love together. My other sister Vanisha had an arranged marriage, and we went to Loughborough to meet her prospective husband and arrange the wedding. I danced a Bollywood dance at their wedding which I was so proud to do for them.

I did another 5 years at Leeds College of technology, I did life skills and work prep. I liked it there because they got me a job in admin at Tech North which is a Leeds City Council building. I had to do emails, faxing, taking phone calls and messages.

I now live independently in Hyde Park; I've been here 10 years. I really enjoy living independently and doing my own thing. My favourite hobbies are going on computers, Bollywood dancing and singing and I support Leeds United football club. Me and my girlfriend Colleen like the same players especially number 10 Alioski.

My best friends include many of the Café Leep trainees who are also people with a learning disability who I train with. Leep1 members are all like a family to me, the staff are like my brothers and sisters. I'm also good friends with my family and cousin. My amazing girlfriend Colleen is one of my best friends and is one of the AND entrepreneurs whom we mention in chapter 6. I will always love her from the bottom of my heart. She helped me through many hard times through lockdown. She has supported me with my diet, and we are always there for each other. The best thing about the AND team is that we can all put forward our ideas. I introduced my culture into AND by drawing my Hindu hand paints. We all have lots of fun and we make each other laugh. It is important for people with learning disabilities as it gives us work experience and shows people around the world that we can achieve things in our lives. Being an entrepreneur makes me feel happy and proud. It means I am an inspiration to others. In the future I hope that AND wins awards. I want to make a difference and educate people on my religion and do more meditation. Meditation helps me to relax my mind from my worries.

I want more people to join AND from different cultures. I want to listen to other people's stories who have learning disabilities. At AND I have learnt art skills, IT skills and teamwork skills. It has helped me to become more confident and positive and allowed me to express my spirituality and be more relaxed. Amanda and Rob have been so helpful and I'm happy they let me onto the AND team. Amanda always makes me laugh and puts a smile on my face. Rob has been helpful and introduced me to different music. My favourite bit of the project was designing the hand henna painting, it is called mehndi in Hindu. It is important to me as it shows my spirituality and introduces my culture. Mehndi is used in Diwali Festival of Light and at Hindu weddings. I love going to Diwali Festival of Light, so it was important for me to show this in my designs. Working as a team means working with others with equal opportunity and respect. It makes us happy and joyful when we work as a team.

We had a lovely lady who came to our club nights in the city centre at Pryzm, she did henna hand painting which all the clubbers enjoyed getting drawn onto their hands. I especially loved this and cannot wait to see her come again; brides have this done before their weddings.

People like me as I'm a handsome guy that is kind and makes people laugh. I always want to make people happy when they are down. I am there for everyone if they are ever down. Me and Colleen share common interests and support each other unconditionally. I know that everyone at AND are always there for me if I am down. My family is important to me, I always want to make them proud.

We are like a big family at Leep1, and we all make each other laugh. It is important for me to stay positive despite any hard times I go through as I want to make everyone proud. In future I would like to get my story out on the radio and YouTube. I want to get a job in admin for the future. I want to help people with their admin skills on the telephone and on the computer.

I love listening to different types of music, I would love a picture of me and my girlfriend together in this book.

I like working as a team and enjoy helping my team mates to reach our goal.

Our goal is the AND – Abilities Not Disabilities to get our voices heard so that other people with learning disabilities can do the same things and have the same opportunities.

Being at Leep1 is important to me, my family are also important, along with my artwork.

In the future I want to be able to carry on being a travel ambassador for Leeds City Council. It is important to me I can show other people how to become independent on transport such as buses.

Photo Credit: Jan Wells

CHAPTER 6

COLLEEN WARD

Photo Credit: Jan Wells – Colleen modelling Bhupesh's Indian design at Leeds canal

My name is Colleen, I am 30 years old, I live with my mum in Whinmoor in Leeds, I have lived here for the last 20 years. I have one older sister and my brother is the youngest.

I went to school at John Smeatons Academy, my best friends at school were called Matthew and Jessica. I met my very first boyfriend called Johnathon at school, we were together for quite a lot of years. We visited each other's houses, and he came on my birthday. At school my favourite lesson was PE because we played Tennis and Rounders which I loved.

After I left John Smeatons school, I went to Horsforth college, here I used to do life skills and did level 3 in animal care. We looked after the guinea pigs, tortoises, and purple snakes. We had to be in our lessons on time otherwise we would get a warning. My best friends at college were Bethany, Alexandra, and Ella, we always had a good laugh together.

After college I became a member of Leep1, when I first started there, I was terribly shy, I used to put my head down and my hands over my face. My confidence grew within the first few months, and I really loved making friends with the members there. Everybody was so nice to me, I felt so welcomed by everyone.

I became a trainee in Café Leep on a Friday, and they taught me about food safety and customer service skills. I was one of the top learners because I always took home the test sheets to revise to pass my food safety exam. I asked Darren the trainer to set me homework every week.

I was in Café Leep for around two years, and I passed my level 2 food safety exam and went on to find employment at The Owl pub in the heart of the Leeds Market. When I did my first day, I was nervous but once I got used to it, it became easier. I was so excited to get my first wage, the first thing I did with it was buy myself some chocolates and a Leeds United top. It makes me proud getting a wage every month.

I love being part of the AND project as I love art and design. My sunflower design I chose to draw was inspired by the artist Vincent Van Gough. It feels amazing that my design is on bags for people to buy.

I loved doing my first photo shoot it made me feel happy and positive and I loved posing in the new designs.

In the future I want to keep my job in The Owl as I love being a bar maid and pulling pints which is my favourite thing to do.

My boyfriend is one of the entrepreneurs and we met through the AND project. We go lots of places together which we enjoy, and he is always there for me, full of jokes and very caring.

My favourite hobby is watching films on DVD and Disney and reading books, I love going for long walks with my dogs and my mum. My mum is the best in the world.

I received the 'Healthy Eating' Award in lockdown for posting my healthy meals daily and doing lots of steps when I was out and about. I lost 2 and a half stone in weight which is an incredible achievement.

CHAPTER 7

ASHLEY

Hi, my name is Ashley, I grew up in Leeds. I went to Quarry Mount Primary School then I went to secondary school at Lawnswood. I enjoyed school and liked the lessons, especially the English classes. I had lots of friends in school. I went to college in Morley, studying english, art and cooking. I liked the lessons at college and had lots of friends. Growing up, I lived with my mum dad and older sister Carrie. She now lives with her two sons in Leeds, and I still live with my mum and dad in the home we grew up in. My favourite hobbies include yoga, drawing, music, and cooking. My best friend is Chops my cat; he is a ginger cat who often appears in the zoom calls I have with my friends at LEEP1.

The best thing about being in the AND team is the fact I get to do art. I like that the things I have designed are now on sale in shops. Learning to be an entrepreneur has meant I have learnt many skills that I am hoping to use in the future. I would love to carry on being a great designer for AND and continue to be involved in this amazing project in the future. Skills I have learnt in AND include making decisions that benefit the project. It has also meant my drawing skills have improved and developed. AND has helped me build my confidence.

This is my first time working with Amanda and Rob. It is exciting to work with Amanda as she is a fantastic artist and helps everyone at AND a lot. It is also fun to work with Rob. I like how he develops the social media for AND and helps the project. My favourite part of AND is the artwork. I really enjoyed helping to create the window installation for Fabrication. The reason I enjoy working as a team is because I like the support that being in a team provides. I like working with others to create the clothes and the window installation.

People like me because I am kind, polite and hardworking. I am also the Kahoot quiz champion! As well as this, I am caring and a great cat owner. There are lots of things that are very important to me. These include LEEP1 and the AND project. Family is also very important to me – my mum dad, sister, and nephews. These things will continue to be important to me. In the future my ideal job would be a chef for a restaurant. The AND project has given me many skills to be able to reach my future goals.

Photo credit: Jan Wells

CHAPTER 8

ENTREPRENEUR STORY – ANNETTE

Photo credit: Jan Wells

My name is Annette Probets, I'm 32 and I grew up in Kent and then moved to Leeds when I was quite young. Growing up I lived with my mum, dad and two brothers. Unfortunately, my mum has now passed away, but my dad is still living, he lives with his new partner now. My brother also moved into supported living; he also has a learning disability. I am very close to this brother, and I get to see him regularly.

I enjoyed my time at school in Kent, I can't remember the name of the school. My brother went to the same school as me and I often saw him there. My favourite lessons at school were maths.

After school finished, we had moved to Leeds, I went to college in Dewsbury, it was on top of Dewsbury Hill. I liked it at college as I had many friends there, my best friend was Ashley who I no longer see but I still speak to her on WhatsApp. She now has her own family; and she doesn't have a learning disability. I did woodwork at college, I made bird tables, tables and loved working with wood.

I now live in a supported living home; I really enjoy living in supported living as I now have my own independence. I have my own bedroom which is nice and peaceful, and staff knock when they want to speak with me. I also get to meet up with my friends, some of my best friends are Joe, Darren, Chris, Jamie, and Colleen. I meet up with Joe often and he makes me laugh which I love. My hobbies include swimming, cooking, art, and music. My favourite thing to do is interact with my friends using my computer. I love typing on my computer and my skills are improving every day.

I entered the Special Olympics, the races I entered were back stroke and front stroke. I came first in a few races which I got a medal for, I was so proud at the time. I trained hard for this every Wednesday evening at Kirkstall swimming baths. Leep1 came to support me and cheer me on, it was a great feeling to know my friends were supporting me and cheering me on from the balcony.

I absolutely love to cook all sorts of food, my passion for cooking started when I became a trainee working in Café Leep. My job at Café LEEP is very important to me and I am currently doing my food hygiene NVQ 2. Working in Café LEEP has given me the key skills and confidence needed to work in the kitchen in schools. I plan to carry on working towards my goal of working in a school kitchen and working amongst young children which I absolutely love.

I always wanted to work as a nursery nurse as I love working with infant children, they bring me so much joy. Hopefully, I will be able to when I work in the school kitchens, serving their dinners to them.

I now cook at home on a regular basis, the things I learnt to cook are chicken and chorizo pasta bake, lasagne, chilli, bolognese, risotto and many more recipes. I am also a fantastic baker and I have run my own baking sessions on our Leep1 Facebook group page online. I did this on Facebook live and had lots of people watching me bake and bake along with me at the same time. I do banana and blueberry muffins, brownies, and a Victoria sponge with fruit on top. I even arrange food in my fridge at home in the correct order that I was taught in Café Leep and have different coloured boards at home too, green for vegetables, red for raw meat, brown for potatoes, white for dairy and yellow for cooked meat.

My favourite thing about the AND team is that I get to see my friends and work with them to create amazing designs. I feel proud knowing that I have helped create the AND project. Learning how to become an entrepreneur has given me many skills for me to use in the future. It has helped me improve my art, work as a team, helped my computer skills and I have learnt how to run a business. It has also boosted my confidence and helps me to speak with others.

I have worked with Amanda previously at Café LEEP and she is good to be around. Rob is very helpful and makes me laugh. Whilst on the AND project, I have loved drawing and painting from home. I loved doing the photoshoot and modelling all the different designs. We have done many art projects and designs working together as a team. It makes me feel happy and accomplished when we come together to do different projects.

Many people think I am a kind and caring person. I am a good friend to Joe; he enjoys spending time with me and thinks I'm funny. My family and friends are important to me as well as continuing to be an amazing designer for AND.

CHAPTER 9

JOE BOOTH

Hi, my name is Joe, I'm 30 years old, I grew up in Rawdon in Leeds, I lived with my mum and sister growing up. My sister is 36 and now lives in Pudsey with her cat.

I went to Rawdon Littlemoor Primary; My favourite lesson was English; I didn't really like any of the other lessons much. I went there till I was about 11, I then went to Ralph Thorsby High School, I didn't really enjoy school. My favourite thing about this school was IT and History. I got my GCSE, but I can't remember what they were in.

I moved from Rawdon when I was 15 and from there, I went into supported living in Armley. Supported living is when I live independently with support. I enjoyed living independently for a long time but more recently I moved to Bramley because I didn't like where I lived towards the end. The new home I now live in I really like the new house I live in now because it is more supportive, and the staff are helpful. I get to do more of the things I choose to do now, and I much prefer it.

From age 16 to 19, I went to Thomas Danby college to do a

catering course; we had our own café which we ran during lunch times for all the members of staff. I did cooking, serving, cleaning and washing up.

From leaving college I got involved in Café Leep which I spoke about in chapter 1. First, I became a trainee in the café in 2015 and was a trainee for about 2 years. During this time, I passed my NVQ 2 in food safety, my pass rate was 97% and everyone and myself were proud of this achievement.

Because of this I was asked to volunteer within the café mentoring other trainees that came on the course. More recently, I have been employed by Café Leep during lockdown which I am very proud of. To be in paid employment it gives me a sense of purpose and a reason to get out of bed. Because I was employed by Leep1 I was able to design an employment e-booklet which will support learning-disabled and autistic adults into and beyond employment. This booklet will help many into employment which is something that had been needed for a long time. We designed and shaped the booklet; it is in an accessible format and can be used widely for other learning-disabled and autistic adults.

I now mentor the trainees in the café and make sure they know what they are doing, I also help with cooking orders that come in.

My best friend is Annette; however, I work with such a wonderful team and have some amazing friends. My favourite hobbies are going and socialising with friends, I love to go bowling, cinema, and sometime nice meals.

I love seeing my family, it was hard over lockdown not seeing everyone but now this is easing I can get to meet up with them and spend some quality time.

I got involved in AND right from the beginning, this was because of my involvement with the prototype clothing that was launched back in 2019. I was one of the original models for the clothing and was excited when I was asked by Amanda to become one of the entrepreneurs helping to shape the business.

Photo credit: Jan Wells

We started the project working with the other 7 entrepreneurs in January 2021 and we work brilliantly as a team.

We talked about what was needed to run an online business and started developing our ideas and artwork for the project. Over the weeks we grew in confidence as a team, I feel the area that I really developed in was doing the social media marketing. When the project finishes, I want to become a social media marketeer.

We have just recently modelled the new designs which I really enjoyed; it was great to see the final pictures of the photo shoot, I'm really proud of our work so far.

I'm excited to see the development of the project and being part of the consultation group who will be developing the safe shopping app. This will change the world for many learning-disabled and autistic adults across the UK and possibly beyond.

CHAPTER 10

SALLY PATER

Model shoot at Leeds canal, May 2021

Photo credit: Jan Wells

Hi, my name is Sally, I'm 41. I have a younger sister and a dad, and I'm engaged to my partner Mark. I lived in Coventry until I was three years old and lived with my mum and dad. I then moved up North and eventually settled in Leeds in my thirties and I now live in Rothwell.

I went to Salters Gate first and middle school from age 5 right up till around the age of 11/12. My favourite teacher was the headteacher called Mr Limes because he was lovely and wasn't strict and you could really have a good laugh with him. I stayed for school dinners every day which were average.

My best friends at school were Debbie and Louise and we got on well. My favourite lesson was French, and I can count to 40 and say my name in French.

I went to Ridgewood, which was a mainstream school, I enjoyed going to school. I loved doing the cooking lessons because it gave independent skills. I didn't have many friends in this school, and I didn't have a good time because I was bullied.

After I left Ridgewood, I went to college, which was in Doncaster, here I learned Drama, painting and decorating and life skills.

Since leaving I gained employment, I worked in Morrison's in Doncaster, it was good but made me very tired. I worked with Stephanie who I like a lot. I worked on the salad bar.

After Morrisons, I got a job in McDonalds then shortly after that I got a job at Doncaster Advocacy where I was able to speak up on behalf of other people. I attended meetings and prepared things so they were ready to start, and I was able to speak up for people who couldn't speak up for themselves.

I got involved in the volunteering for all project and travelled to Leeds to do this and became a member of HFT. They supported me on a one-to-one basis to help me in the home.

I met my boyfriend in Leeds, and we met in Tiger Tiger, we sat next to each other the whole time and chatted all night. There was a spark between us, and I knew he was the man for me instantly.

The second time I met Mark was our very first proper date, we went to walk around Leeds city centre shopping together. We had to run into a shop because it started to thunder and lightning, and we took shelter as Mark was a bit scared.

I moved out of home because I wanted to become more independent, and my first supported living was not the best because people didn't know how to support me in the right way. Soon after that I moved out and moved to Leeds which was nearer to my boyfriend Mark.

I lived with another lady, but we didn't get on very well therefore she moved out and HFT helped me to organise for Mark to move in. This made me happy as I love Mark so much, he is my best friend.

I am also the co-chair for the health task group which feeds into the Leeds City Council 'Being Me' strategy which helps make the health service better for learning-disabled and/or autistic adults.

My favourite things to do is art, art makes me feel like I can express myself and I get lost in a world of art. I love to write poetry and stories; I want to read them to more people so they can hear what I have written.

This is one of my poems below;

The silent mind of an autistic lady

An autistic lady masks her feelings because she's worried, she won't be heard or understood.

She means well but believes others can't see that.

The lady who does not want to be identified, cries because she is a person who is expressing herself.

The world is colourful but neuro-typical people can't see her true colours.

Unless they let her shine.

I saw a post on the Leep1 group page, and I applied to become one of the entrepreneurs on the course. I enjoy working with the AND team and love expressing myself through the designs I make. We all work well together, and we are a brilliant team. My art has improved since joining and I have created some incredible designs for AND. I wanted to give them strength and positivity so I used lots of words like peace, strength, and hope in my designs. My second design is a memory for my mum who has passed away, I drew this picture because every time I look at this design it makes me happy.

**Here is one of Sally's designs which is featured in a post-card
pack to purchase online.**

I would love to become a fashion designer when I finish the
AND course, and I would love to eventually get married to Mark. I
have recently started another art course so I can develop my skills in
art even further.

Chapter 11

Bernadette

Hi, my name is Bernadette, I grew up in Temple Newsam in Leeds, I have lived there all my life in the same house which I love.

I went to West Oaks school in Boston Spa. I enjoyed school and went on lot of trips with them. My favourite trip was Cologne in Germany where I stayed with a German family. The food was lovely, I really like Bratwurst which is their version of hot dogs.

Another trip I went on was a climbing trip that was at Atlantic college, we climbed a wall, it was quite scary and when we got to the top it felt good, like I had accomplished a new skill and wasn't as scared of heights because of it. I left college at 19.

After I left, I went to Thomas Danby College where I studied catering and waitress service. My best friend at college was Aysha. The best thing I enjoyed was the waitress service because I like to help and serve people. I got to work behind the bar within the college on the night-time which I loved as I got to use my customer service skills. I left college with my NVQ 2 and 3 in catering which made me feel proud.

I went on to do the cooking course run by Ministry of Food

which is situated in the heart of Leeds Market. This course taught me more cooking skills which I was able to use at home.

At home I live with my dad, I have 1 older sister and 2 nephews who live in Wetherby, I love visiting my sister every week.

My hobbies are art, and my favourite is watercolours, I like to do colouring books to help me relax. I also enjoy jigsaws, horse riding and cooking.

I love coming to Leep1 and everyone is my friend. My best friends are Colleen and Susan, and we do video chats together.

I like being part of the AND team and being able to do lots of art. Being able to sell my work makes me feel good and proud. It's important to learn new skills and understand how the business works.

I would love to be an artist and show others how to draw and use watercolours. My artwork skills have got better since I joined the AND team.

Being with my friends helps my confidence and improves my art and being able to sell my artwork makes me feel confident. Doing the photoshoot made me feel proud and I can't wait to do some more modelling.

Photo credit: Jan Wells

Here is Bernie's Toucan design currently for sale on a tote bag.

Her beautiful watercolour design has some awesome detail on it.

Here is all our merchandise currently on sale.

Scan with your camera and it will bring up the AND website automatically with all the AND designs.

Here is our AND Facebook page with all the latest updates on our entrepreneurs.

Send us a like to show your support.

AND Instagram – follow us

Twitter page – follow us

Thank you for purchasing this book – all proceeds go back into supporting more entrepreneurs through the programme and raises more awareness of how society needs to be more inclusive, kind and open more doors to employment for this community of talented individuals.

A special thanks to Jan Wells who took the brilliant pictures of our entrepreneurs she has done some amazing work putting together a media portfolio to show off AND to it's full potential.

Printed in Great Britain
by Amazon